⌐. ∪∟⌐ι∨ι∟Ɐ

REVIEWS FROM READERS

I recently downloaded a couple of books from this series to read over the weekend thinking I would read just one or two. However, I so loved the books that I read all the six books I had downloaded in one go and ended up downloading a few more today. Written by different authors, the books offer practical advice on how you can perform or achieve certain goals in life, which in this case is how to have a better life.

The information is simple to digest and learn from, and is incredibly useful. There are also resources listed at the end of the book that you can use to get more information.

50 Things To Know To Have A Better Life: Self-Improvement Made Easy!

Author Dannii Cohen

This book is very helpful and provides simple tips on how to improve your everyday life. I found it to be useful in improving my overall attitude.

50 Things to Know For Your Mindfulness & Meditation Journey
Author Nina Edmondso

Quick read with 50 short and easy tips for what to think about before starting to homeschool.

50 Things to Know About Getting Started with Homeschool by Author Amanda Walton

I really enjoyed the voice of the narrator, she speaks in a soothing tone. The book is a really great reminder of things we might have known we could do during stressful times, but forgot over the years.

Author HarmonyHawaii

---

50 Things to Know to Manage Your Stress: Relieve The Pressure and Return The Joy To Your Life

Author Diane Whitbeck

There is so much waste in our society today. Everyone should be forced to read this book. I know I am passing it on to my family.

50 Things to Know to Downsize Your Life: How To Downsize, Organize, And Get Back to Basics

Author Lisa Rusczyk Ed. D.

Great book to get you motivated and understand why you may be losing motivation. Great for that person who wants to start getting healthy, or just for you when you need motivation while having an established workout routine.

50 Things To Know To Stick With A Workout: Motivational Tips To Start The New You Today

Author Sarah Hughes

50 THINGS TO KNOW ABOUT BEING A ZOOKEEPER

LIFE OF A ZOOKEEPER

Stephanie Fowlie

Cover designed by: Ivana Stamenkovic
Cover Image: https://pixabay.com/photos/sealion-sea-lion-female-sea-lion-4339210/

CZYK Publishing Since 2011.

50 Things to Know

Lock Haven, PA
All rights reserved.
ISBN: 9798677174124

50 THINGS TO KNOW ABOUT

BOOK DESCRIPTION

Have you dreamed of a career where you can work with exotic animals? Have you ever wanted to better understand the day to day tasks of caring for wild animals? Do you want to make a difference in an animal's life?

If you answered yes to any of these questions, then this 50 Things to Know book is for you.

50 Things to Know about Becoming a Zookeeper by Stephanie Fowlie offers an approach to understanding what zookeeping entails and other similar zoo jobs. Most books on zookeeping tell you about the history of zoos and aquariums and basic tasks of the zookeeper. Although there's nothing wrong with that, there is more to becoming a zookeeper than just knowing the basics. Based on knowledge from the world's leading experts this book will help you decide if becoming a zookeeper is the right choice for you.

In these pages you will discover everything from education to salary to the importance of zoos. This book will help you decide if becoming a zookeeper is the right path for you.

By the time you finish his book, you will know what needs to be done in order to become a zookeeper. So grab YOUR copy today. You'll be glad you did.

TABLE OF CONTENTS

DEDICATION

This book is dedicated to my parents, Lynn and Ken, who have always supported my dreams no matter how crazy they may seem.

ABOUT THE AUTHOR

Stephanie Fowlie recently graduated from Unity College in May 2020. She majored in Captive Wildlife Care and Education with a minor in zoology and has dreamed of working with animals since she was a little girl. She even went to an agricultural high school where she majored in Small Animal Science.

Stephanie continuously volunteers at her local animal shelter and hopes to become a full-time zookeeper in the near future. In her free time Stephanie loves spending time with her family, making new friends, and reading her growing collection of books.

She is currently residing in Massachusetts where she lives in her childhood home. She has three cats, Chewie, Vader, and Orion, and two dogs, Max and Otis who all mean the world to her.

Where you find you on social media… Instagram: Steph_Fowlie

INTRODUCTION

*"People forget the good that
zoos do. If it weren't for zoos, we
would have so many species that
would be extinct today."*

Betty White

A zookeeper is someone who cares for the animals in a zoo. Some people tend to think that a zookeeper's job is just cleaning up after the animals. Though that is a big part of the job, zookeeping is much more than just cleaning up poop.

Zookeepers have many daily tasks that include feeding, cleaning, and reporting any health problems to the vet. They will also usually have other tasks such as educating the public and record keeping. On occasion zookeepers will also be involved in scientific research at the facility.

As a zookeeper, you need to be able to work well with the animals in your care and the people around you. A zookeeper needs to be able to bond with the animals so that they can pick up on any abnormal behaviors (working with the animals every day makes

5

it easy to form bonds with the animals). The keeper –
animal relationship is a big part of the job though that
does not mean that zookeepers get to sit around and
play with animals all day. Zookeepers need to be able
to work closely with other keepers, supervisors, and
the public so communication (both spoken and
written) is very important. The following tips will go
over everthing I wish I knew as I was choosing my
career and going through school.

EDUCATION

1. START EARLY/ELEMENTARY SCHOOL

The earlier you start preparing for a career as a
zookeeper the better off you will be! In elementary
school it is important to do as much research about
animals as possible. You can watch nature
documentaries, read books and magazines, and take
trips to the zoo and aquarium. *National Geographic*
and *Animal Planet* were always my favorite channels
to watch growing up!

Taking nature hikes, visiting parks, and natural
history museums can also allow you the chance to

learn more about wildlife. You can also ask your parents if you can have a pet. This will help you learn about the responsibilities of animal care. If your school has a science club be sure to join it and if you have the chance to join scouting activities take it! When you are outdoors stop for a moment and observe the wildlife. Keep a nature journal with you so that you will be able to write down all of these observations. You can even bring a guidebook to help you identify the animals you see. Lastly, make sure to work hard in school! Though most of the related classes are science based, not all of them are. Any projects that I had that I could choose my topic I chose something that was about animals; I remember doing a project on Giant Panda's when I was in elementary school! You want to keep up your grades and learn as much as you can in all of your classes.

2. MIDDLE/SECONDARY SCHOOL

Once you are in secondary school you want to continue to research about animals and observing them when you are outside. Make sure you continue to do all of the things mentioned in the previous tip (or start them if you haven't already!). The animal

7

care field is continuously changing so it is important to stay up to date on what is going on, after all, there is always more to learn! If you are old enough to get a part-time job or volunteer you will want to find something at a pet shop, animal shelter, a veterinary hospital, or something similar to start gaining hands on experience with animal care in a professional setting. When I was in middle school was when I started looking at high schools and careers that allowed me to work with animals (for a long time I wanted to be a vet but in middle school I changed to wanting to become a zookeeper).

3. HIGH SCHOOL

High school is a good time to let your teachers and guidance counselor know what you are planning on doing as a career. They can help you work out a schedule so that you can learn as much as possible in the animal care field. If you are like me and you have access to an agricultural high school with an animal science department, go there! This will allow you to start learning about animal related topics and possibly get hands on experience with animals. In my high school classes I took courses like dog grooming, vet science, and Animal ethics. Of course, make sure to continue doing the things mentioned in the previous two tips or start them if you haven't already! I started volunteering at my local animal shelter in high school and I still do today! High School is also the time to start looking for colleges. When looking at colleges try to find somewhere that specializes in biology, zoology, animal husbandry, ecology, veterinary medicine, ethology, and/or wildlife and forestry. Take any chance you get to visit the schools you are interested and choose which is the best fit for you! Do not be discouraged if you find this choice difficult, it should be! After all this decision is going to affect the rest of your life! I applied to six different schools, visited my top two, and waited to hear back from all of them before making my decision.

4. COLLEGE

Once you choose your college, you want to choose a major and take classes on topics relevant to zookeeping. These topics include, biology, forestry, animal husbandry, animal training, ecology, veterinary medicine, environmental studies, etc. You should get a bachelor's degree in one of the fields mentioned above (some zoos may accept an associate degree). Double majoring or minoring in another related field is also a plus (I minored in zoology). You can also look for a part-time or seasonal job while in college so you can start gaining hands on experience with animals. Remember volunteering is always an option if you cannot get a job! Remember to keep learning all that you can about zookeeping and animals because as mentioned before, the field is constantly changing, and it is important to keep up with all of the new information. One of my college classes was just on finding a new article in the zookeeping field every week and discussing it in class.

5. COURSES

Every school will be different when it comes to courses that are available to take. If you want to focus on a specific type of animal, it is important to find topics specifically about them (if you want to work with birds take an ornithology course etc.). Since my school is an environmental college it was easy to find relevant courses to take. When it comes to looking for a job, many places will look at the courses that you have taken along with the degree that you earned. Take courses that are relevant to zookeeping. Animal related courses are important but courses like public speaking or video editing may be helpful too. Most colleges require you to take an art course, I felt that photography was the most beneficial to me. You are also required to take a certain amount of electives in order to graduate, these courses can of course just be for fun but you should try to take the courses that can help you in your future career.

6. EXPERIENCE

Gaining experience in this field is highly important because most jobs want you to have some experience when you apply. A good way to get experience is to volunteer or find a part-time job working with animals. Another thing to look into once you are in college is internships and externships at zoos, aquariums, wildlife sanctuaries, and/or wildlife rehabilitation centers. Take as many of these opportunities as possible, it will only benefit you in the end! I personally only got the chance to do one internship but I have been volunteering at an animal shelter for about 5 years now.

7. INTERNSHIP

Many colleges require their students to do an internship so that they can start gaining experience in their chosen field. Internships are important because it is a valuable learning experience. For an internship you will usually get college credit, though this sometime depends on the school or where you are doing your internship. This is a great opportunity to learn from professionals and figure out if this is exactly what you want to do for the rest of your life. When I did my internship it helped me realize that I would prefer to work with animals that are free contact because I enjoyed being able to go into the enclosure with the animals I was caring for. Even if your school does not require an internship you should definitely still apply to some. Experience is key in this field, and the more experience you get the better off you will be.

8. EXTERNSHIP

An externship is very similar to an internship except you do not get college credit. Externships should be done after you graduate. This is a great way to get more experience and learn from professionals in this field. You can also have the opportunity to work with different animals then you did during your internship, which will allow you the chance to see if you prefer one or the other. If you maintain a good relationship with the keepers you work with during an externship (or internship) it could potentially lead to a job when the externship is over. I personally have never done an externship but know someone who has and he kept a good relationship with the keepers he was working with and now has a job as a keeper in the same location.

SKILLS

9. KEY SKILLS

Some key skills that you should have when applying for a zookeeper position include, strong decision-making, independent thinking, observation, interpersonal skills, customer service skills, time management, and record keeping skills. It is also important that you can manage animals and perform a certain amount of physical labor. Most places require you to be able to lift at least 50 pounds (food bags can be heavy!). You should also be capable of working in all types of weather and temperatures (if you know that you are not very good in the heat try to find a job up north; summer months will still be hot but most of the year will be colder). There are also some other skills that are not a requirement but may be beneficial to getting a zookeeping job.

10. FIRST AID/CPR

Knowing first aid/CPR in a zoo is important because you work in proximity with other employees and zoo guests and there is always a potential for injuries. One thing to note is that zoos and aquariums have to pay for first aid training for their staff. If you already have first aid training, it is possible that potential employers will see that as a plus since they will not need to pay for that training. A bonus is that first aid training is helpful in everyday life too! So even if you never need it during your career it may be useful at some point in your life. A pet first aid certification can look good on a resume as well! The same basic techniques for pet first aid apply to human first aid; you would still need to go through both certificate processes but they both look good on resumes and will only benefit you!

11. SCUBA/BOAT LICENSE

If you are working with terrestrial species, then this tip does not apply to you. These qualifications are, however, important if you will be working with aquatic species. There are some aquariums that will not hire people who do not have a SCUBA license so you should do as much research beforehand to see if you will need one or not. It should also be noted that not every position in an aquarium will need a SCUBA license. A boat license can be important if you are working on research or rehabilitation and rescue within the zoo or aquarium.

12. COMPUTER SKILLS

Almost nothing is kept on hard copy anymore; most zoos use computers for record keeping. Understanding basic computer skills and Microsoft functions are important to effectively do this part of the job. You may be able to take a course on computer skills though if you grew up around technology this skill may come easy to you. There is even a database for AZA accredited zoos with details about all of the breeding animals in captivity (this is called a studbook). This database is used to ensure that species are healthy and genetically diverse. You may even want to know the basics of video and picture editing for the facility's social media pages which is commonly used for public outreach.

13. INTERPERSONAL SKILLS

Having interpersonal skills is important to be successful as a zookeeper. Zookeepers consistently communicate with other keepers and to their superiors to provide the best care possible for the animals in the facility. You get great practice with this skill as an intern since you need to communicate with the keepers that you are working with often. This skill can also be learned from other jobs and during group projects in school. Having good interpersonal skills helps you become a leader by taking ownership of projects while showing empathy for coworkers and the animals in your care.

14. PROBLEM-SOLVING SKILLS

As a zookeeper it is common to be faced with obstacles on the job. It is important to have problem solving skills in this role so that you can efficiently work though these obstacles. One common obstacle can be animals being hidden from view. This sometimes cannot be avoided but you can always try putting enrichment in a viewable spot to attract the animals. Be sure to widen the experiences you have through school and work so you can apply what you have learned once you get a job as a zookeeper.

15. CUSTOMER SERVICE SKILLS

Zookeepers work with the public to educate them about the animals in their care and answer any questions the zoo visitors may have. Many zookeepers also have a daily "keeper chat" to promote education in the zoo. Keeper chats can be about numerous different topics including a certain species or habitat. One keeper chat that I have heard was about palm oil and how it affects our rainforests. During the talk the keeper told the audience how they can help without donating money. Working with the public requires proficient customer service skills so that the visitors experience is favorable. It is also important to note that it is common to come in contact with difficult guests. In one of the bonus tips at the end of this book I explain how to handle these types of people.

16. TIME MANAGEMENT SKILLS

When you are a zookeeper you need to be mindful of the amount of time you spend on each task. Zookeepers have many tasks that need to be done throughout the day and sometimes unexpected problems can occur. A zookeeper should focus on one task at a time, set achievable goals, prioritize tasks based on their importance and delegate tasks to others when necessary. They should also be able to rely on the other keepers when they need help completing certain duties within a timeframe. Always remember that you will get faster at doing the daily tasks the more you do them! It takes time to find a way that is efficient for you and what works for one person may not work well for another.

17. OBSERVATION SKILLS

Observation skills are important to have as a zookeeper because keepers are often the first to realize when an animal is sick. Every morning and even throughout the day keepers do something called a "life-check" to look for any abnormal behaviors. When you spend almost every day caring for the animals it is easy to pick up on any behaviors that do not usually occur. Having good observational skills could possibly save an animal's life. A good example of this is when I was doing my internship. After spending nearly three months with the animals in my area, one afternoon I realized that one of the birds was not eating or flying away like she usually did. We later found out that she had swallowed something and she needed to stay in the clinic for closer observation. Observational skills are also useful when dealing with the public. You need to keep a sharp eye if there is a potential of visitors getting in contact with an animal in your care. One of my daily tasks was to take out our two yellow-footed tortoises so they can get some direct sunlight and exercise. When I did this they were not behind a glass but rather right near where people are. I needed to keep a close eye on the people arpund the tortoises (especially children) so that they did not run up and touch them.

18. PROFESSIONAL CONDUCT

Since you will come in contact with the public daily as a zookeeper it is important to be professional. This includes having a neat uniform with the zoos logo and upholding the professional image of the zoo. There are many zoos that do not allow their employees to have any unnatural hair color, piercings, or visible tattoos. Some jewelry can also be potentially dangerous; jewelry could be grabbed by the animals or caught on something in the exhibit. Always check on the dress code for places you are looking at applying to for these guidelines. Visitors should be able to easily identify the zookeepers so that they can ask them for information or assistance. Not only should a keeper's attire be professional, but their behavior in the workplace should be too (for example respect for others and politeness).

19. KNOW CHARACTERISTICS OF THE ANIMAL KINGDOM

It is important to know about the animals that you are working with. Zoo visitors will often ask the keepers questions about the animals. Education is a big part of zoos and the keepers, whether they are an educational keeper or not, should know the basics about each animal in their care. Common questions that keepers should know the answers to include, what is the life span of the animal, what the species is, where they are found in the wild. You should also know about the individual animal since many people like knowing how old the individual is or what the animals name is. With experience you will start to learn what the common questions asked are. Of course, never be afraid to tell someone that you do not know the answer to a question; it is better than giving a false answer! Then when you get the chance you can look it up and you will know the answer if it is every asked again.

It is also important to understand the natural history of the animals in your care as this will allow you to take care of them to the best of your ability. Each animal needs different food, enrichment, space, family groups etc. Understanding each of these aspects will make the animals live a better life in their captive home. Make sure to stay updated on captive animal news; as mentioned before, this field constantly changes. As more research goes on and we better understand the animals in captivity we may need to adjust their habitats in order to give them a better life.

20. KNOW REPRODUCTIVE BIOLOGY

Knowing reproductive biology of the animals is important for a couple of different reasons. One reason is that zoo visitors may have questions about the reproduction. Another is that many zoos participate in breeding programs (AZA accredited facilities are a part of the species survival plan which is a breeding program for endangered species). Lastly, it could be a good keeper chat topic. For example, I have done a keeper chat about the species survival plan and in order to talk about the species survival plan I needed to talk about the reproduction of the animals in my care. Though I specifically focused on one of the species in my care I briefly mentioned some of the others; so, knowing about the animal's reproductive biology is important to a zookeeper's job.

21. ANIMAL TRAINING

Every keeper should know the basics of how to train animals. You should understand the different types of training and when to use which. Operant conditioning is the basis of animal training. It is when the animal learns from its behaviors as it acts on the environment. During this training, a behavior will happen either more often or less often depending on its results. Positive reinforcement (rewards) is a favorable consequence of an action. There is also negative reinforcement which gives the animal an unfavorable stimulus as a result of an action. When training you want to make sure you start with the basics then add on to the behavior for a more complex behavior. A good starting point is target training. Target training is when you train an animal to touch a body part to an object. Almost any animal can learn to target train, I have even taught a green crab how to! The key is to find a reward that the animal will work for; in the crabs case, I fed him muscles!

It is important to know that every animal picks up differently. Some individuals learn extremely fast, while others are slow learners. One day a training session can go smoothly and the next the animal does not want to cooperate. Make sure to always end a training session on a high note. You want the animal to continue to want to train the next day and ending on a positive note will make training at a later time hopefully go more smoothly. Usually when I'm training I like to gibe the animal a 'jackpot' at the end of the session. A jackpot is when you give the animal multiple rewards rather than just one.

Training the animals in your care is important to help with medical procedures. If an animal is trained to present a body part, step on a scale, or move into a squeeze cage it allows for stress free health checkups. Some common behaviors trained include open mouth (which allows for the vet and keepers to look at an animal's teeth and tongue) and ultrasound training (to check for pregnancy or stomach issues). Training also allows the animal's mind to be stimulated and helps prevent negative behaviors in the animals because of this training is considered to be enrichment. Training sessions also make for good keeper chats and allows for guests to see the animals in a way that they usually do not get to.

22. HABITAT DESIGN

Habitat design aspects such as appropriate furnishings for the species or special considerations must be considered by zookeepers before they accommodate the animal. These mentioned aspects are important because zookeepers are the voice for the animal when it comes to exhibit design. When designing an exhibit, it is important to not only think about the animals, but the zookeepers and the public too. The animals need to be comfortably accommodated in their exhibits, the keepers need to be able to easily clean and maneuver around the exhibits, and the guests need to be able to find the animals within the enclosure. A good exhibit should have a place of shelter for the animals, access to food and water, and enrichment. It would also be ideal for exhibits to have furnishings that could be moved, changing the furnishings every couple of months is a good form of enrichment. If you have a say in the exhibit design do not make it a boring square or rectangle! In one of my classes we built a mock exhibit and my group designed an exhibit for the Madagascar fossa. We built three separate enclosures that was connected by an overhead tunnel. This would allow for the animals to wall overhead zoo

guests. Interesting/different looking exhibits keep
both guests and the animals happy.

23. CONSERVATION ROLES OF ZOOS

Zoos are a great workplace if you are someone
who needs more from a job then just a salary because
zoos help animals. Knowing the missions that zoos
globally help take care of endangered species makes
your daily tasks easier. Zoos were once just for
entertainment but now conservation and education are
two of the most important aspects of zoos around the
world. A zoos mission statement is very important
and it is a good way to figure out if it is a place you
would want to work for. Zoos promote conservation
by education, recycling, research, and donating (or
encouraging guests to donate) to different wildlife
conservation funds.

24. CONSERVATION EDUCATION

Zookeepers need to communicate with both guests and coworkers. Zookeepers not only care for the animals at the facility but are educators. Keepers often have keeper chats to inspire the public to help these endangered species. Keeper chats can be about an individual animal, species, or exhibit (really anything you put your mind too!). These chats often occur during an animal's feeding so that visitors have a better chance at seeing the animal. Though it can be common for a keeper chat to occur when an animal is training too. It is a great chance to talk to zoo visitors about a topic that you are passionate about and the audience gets the chance to ask any questions they have.

THE GOOD AND BAD

25. POSITIVES AND NEGATIVES OF THE JOB

Every career that you look into will have some positives and some negatives. It is up to you to decide if the positives outweigh the negatives of the career.

Some positives of becoming a zookeeper include animal interactions and job stability. Some negatives of becoming a zookeeper is the hard work and potential danger. It is also important to note that this career does not have a high paying salary. When people want to become zookeepers it is because they are passionate about animals and want to help them in any way possible. The unfortunate truth is that if you want to become rich this is not a job that will allow you to do that. The next few tips will go into some more depth of each of these positives and negatives.

26. ANIMAL INTERACTIONS

As a zookeeper you will get the chance for as much direct and indirect animal interaction as a career. Some of the many duties of a zookeeper include feeding and bathing the animals in your care. Monitoring and addressing animal health issues is also a big responsibility of a zookeeper. Sometimes zookeepers even hand raise baby animals. One of my favorite things about being a zookeeper is bonding with the animals in your career. Being able to work closely with them almost every single day allows you to learn each individual's personality just like you would a pets. One thing that I loved doing was seeing the baby animals grow up. When I started my internship the baby Titi Monkey was only a few months old and was very afraid of the keepers. By the end of my internship the baby started to take the food from my hands when I was doing my morning life checks.

27. JOB STABILITY

Though the pay of zookeepers is not very high, job stability is a benefit. Zoos, aquariums, and wildlife preserves usually grow as governments develop conservation programs. With these facilities growing, more jobs start to become available. A zookeeper is a career, not just a job.

28. HARD WORK

A zookeeper will spend much of their day on the move. They need to be able to lift equipment and food bags/pails (usually up to 50 pounds), move animals, and clean exhibits (which sometimes requires bending and/or climbing). Animals require care during the hot or cold, rain or shine. It is common for zookeepers to work weekends and holidays because animals need care every day. Even if the zoo is closed to the public the zookeepers still need to come in to feed and clean up after the animals. You should expect to work long hours, especially during the summer which is the busy season for zoos. During the summer it is common for zoos to hold after hour events that keeper staff are expected to work. The zoo I did my internship at hosted a couple of weddings during the summer amd held multiple after hour zoo events that a handful of the keepers worked.

29. DANGER

Zookeeping can be a dangerous job. As a zookeeper you will most likely be taking care of wild animals, unless you are working in the farm animals' area that most zoos have. No matter the species of animal you are working with though, there is always a chance of injury. Like a past teacher always told me, if it has teeth it can bite and if it has claws it can scratch. Animals can also become sick and spread diseases to the keepers working with them. You should always use caution when working with animals; be observant and be careful. Every animal is potentially dangerous to work with; even after years of working with an animal you need to remember that it is still wild and cam potentially cause injury.

30. SALARY

When finding a job, a common question asked is what is the salary? The median salary for zookeepers in 2020 is $33,519 annually. Just like any other job, the starting pay is lower than the pay of someone in a higher position with more experience. The salary also depends on the individual zoo or aquarium and the location of the facility. Be sure to do research when job searching to find a facility that works for you and do not let this salary stop you from following your passion.

31. DIFFERENT POSITIONS AVAILABLE

As a zookeeper there are opportunities for different positions within the zoo or aquarium. These positions require different levels of experience and sometimes different education needs. Choosing which position is right for you is incredibly important. If you want to work in a zoo or aquarium, you do not need to become a keeper or aquarist to do so. The next few tips will go into more detail about the different positions that are available within a zoo or aquarium.

32. KEEPER/AQUARIST

A keeper/aquarist's job is to care for the animals at the facility. There are many duties that a keeper must be able to do in order to care for the animals properly. These duties include feeding the animals, administrating medication, cleaning and maintaining the exhibits, reporting any unusual behaviors to a veterinarian, assisting with veterinary procedures, and keeping records. It is common for keepers to specialize in a specific area, such as working with birds or big cats though this is not a requirement. It is also common for keepers who are just starting out to get moved from area to area within a facility and to sometimes even move to a totally different facility all together. All keeper positions have the most direct contact with the animals at the facility.

33. PROGRAM ANIMAL KEEPER

Program animal keepers take care of the program animals at the facility. Program animals are the animals used for education purposes. Not only do these keepers need to do the jobs that a normal keeper does, like clean and feed the animals, but they often have educational programs throughout the day. These programs allow zoo visitors to get a closer look at some of the animals and ask questions about the species or individual animals. Sometimes these keepers will bring some program animals to a school to educate young kids by bringing the animals to them. These keepers are also usually the ones in charge of summer camps for kids. Summer camps usually consists of kids of varying ages learning about the animals at the zoo through close encounters and fun activities. Program animals can come in a variety of different species. They can be mammals (rabbits, ferrets, fox, etc.), birds (owls, crows, etc.), reptiles, or even insects.

34. HEAD KEEPER/AQUARIST

A head keeper/aquarist supervises a section or department of the institution. They provide training and scheduling for keepers in their section. Other than the fact that they are responsible for the other keepers in their area, the head keeper/aquarist will have the same responsibilities as the other keepers/aquarists.

35. SENIOR KEEPER/AQUARIST

Senior keepers/aquarists are the keepers/aquarists that provide primary animal care for a department. To become a senior keeper, you will usually have to have many years of keeper experience. It could also be beneficial to have an education background studying whichever area you want to become a senior keeper for (reptiles you should study herpetology etc.).

36. NUTRITIONIST

Zoo nutritionists are in charge of the nutritional management for all animals at the zoo. They are responsible for ensuring that each animal consumes a well-balanced diet with the proper caloric content. They will also adjust the diets for animals that gain or lose weight, animals that are pregnant or lactating, animals that have been ill, or animals that are new and transitioning to the facilities dietary program. It is important to note that smaller zoos do not have a nutritionist and these duties fall onto the keepers. It is also important to note that nutrionists usually will not interact directly with the animals.

37. CONSERVATION BIOLOGIST/ZOOLOGIST

A conservation biologist or zoologist provides scientific and technical assistance in the management of the animal collection. They also assist in conducting various research or field conservation projects. Research is very important in zoos because it helps us better understand the animals we are caring for. It also allows us to make adjustments to conservation efforts both in captivity and in the wild. A conservation biologist or zoologist may specialize in a branch of the field with a related group of animals, such as mammalogy (mammals) or herpetology (reptiles).

38. VETERINARIAN/VET TECH

The veterinarian and vet tech are responsible for providing healthcare to the animals at the facility. The vet will also maintain the health records regarding all the animals in the facility. The vet tech assists the veterinarian in the care of the animals. If a zoo is small, they may not have a vet tech. Though a zoo vet/vet techs main duty are treating the ill or injured animals, there is also a chance that they are involved in research studies or interacting with the public as part of educational events (sometimes these educational events are after hours or apart of the summer camps). If there is only one vet at a zoo they are always on call in case of an emergency.

39. ZOO DIRECTOR

Zoo directors lead the management team that oversees zoo operations. They usually manage park operations, create budgets, implement policies, hire management staff, source additional funding, and oversee the development of the facility. It is common for the zoo director to work closely with the curators in order to keep the facility running smoothly. This position usually does not directly interact with the animals.

40. GENERAL CURATOR

The zoo curator is responsible for managing the animals and staff at the facility. The general curator oversees the entire animal collection, staff, and completes various administrative tasks. In order to become a curator, general or otherwise, you need to have been a keeper/aquarist beforehand. Curators have a higher salary compared to keepers/aquarists. At a smaller zoo the general curator may be the only curator. This position will have limited direct contact with the animals.

41. ANIMAL CURATOR

Like a general curator, an animal curator manages the animal collection at a facility. The animal curator may manage all the animals or some of them depending on the size of the facility. If they only manage some of the collection the animal curators will usually be split into different areas like, curator of mammals or curator of rainforest species. Like the general curator, the animal curator will have limited direct contact with the animals in their care.

JOB LOCATIONS

42. WHERE TO WORK

Deciding the best facility for you to work in can be a challenge. Zookeepers have the choice to work in many different locations including a zoo, aquarium, wildlife rehabilitation center, or a wildlife sanctuary. You should always make sure to do your research about the facilities where you can potentially find a job. The next few tips will go into more detail about different facility types to help you choose which is the right fit for you; there will also be a tip going into detail on how to decipher a bad facility from a good one.

43. ZOO

A zoo is a park where live animals are exhibited. Most zoos house terrestrial species with maybe a few aquatic species, depending on how big the facility is. If you are looking to work with elephants or monkeys (amongst many other different exotic species) a zoo is the right place for you. Working at a zoo will probably give you the most variety of animals to work with compared to a sanctuary. I personally did my internship at a smaller zoo and worked in the rainforest area (the area that has the greatest diversity at th facility). I worked with numerous small primates, birds, and reptiles. There was about 15 different animal species that I worked with on a daily basis.

44. AQUARIUM

An aquarium is a public place where fish and other aquatic animals are exhibited. Aquariums house, fish, sea reptiles (like sea turtles), marine mammals, and sea birds. If you want to work with marine animals, you should look for a job in an aquarium. If you choose to work at an aquarium it is good to keep in mind one of the earlier tips; you may need a SCUBA certificate and/or a boating license.

45. WILDLIFE REHABILITATION

When it comes to wildlife rehabilitation, you can either work at a wildlife rehab center or sometimes zoos and aquariums will rehabilitate animals. It is common for big facilities to have a rehabilitation center along with the zoo/aquarium. Wildlife rehabbers need to be educated in wildlife medicine since most of their duties include taking care of injured or sick wildlife. It is important to note that animal death is a major part of wildlife rehabilitation and it is common for wildlife rehabilitation centers to turn down helping invasive species. Wildlife rehabilitators take care of native wildlife species; if you want to work with exotic species this is probably not the right fit for you.

46. WILDLIFE SANCTUARY

A wildlife sanctuary is a place built for captive animals that become unwanted for various reasons (animals that were kept illegaly etc.). It is common for animals to go to a sanctuary when roadside zoos or circuses run out of business and can no longer care for the animals. The sanctuaries provide care for neglected and abused captive animals for the rest of their lives. They do not breed or sell the animals; when an animal comes to a wildlife sanctuary they stay there until they die of natural causes. Usually wildlife sanctuaries specialize in a certain species of animal rather than having numerous different species. For example there are many big cat sanctuaries throughout the United States and there is an elephant sanctuary in Tennessee.

47. GOOD FACILITIES VS BAD FACILITIES

When it comes to zoos, if the facility is AZA accredited then it will be on the good facility list. Just because a zoo is not accredited though, does not mean that it is a bad facility. The Pittsburgh zoo actually backed out of their accreditation when the AZA changed their standards from being able to work free contact with elephants to working protected contact with elephants because the keepers wanted to continue to work free contact; the Pittsburgh zoo is still one of the best facilities in the United States even without an AZA accreditation. Checking if a facility is non-profit will help you determine if it is a good facility. True non-profit facilities are not just trying to make a profit and get rich, they care about the animals and the zoos mission. Speaking of zoo missions, every zoo will make their mission statement public. Read the mission and educate yourself on what the facility stands for. The mission statement from the zoo that I interned at is "dedicated to preserving the future of wildlife by creating engaging and educational experiences that connect the community to the natural world". Mission statements at good zoos will be very similar to this one. Lastly, make sure there are indicators of good welfare practices. Comfortable living space for animals (food, water, shelter, clean), naturalistic habitats, and enrichment are all important aspects needed for an animal to have a good life.

FINDING A JOB

48. WRITING YOUR RESUME

When you write your resume, you want to make sure you list those key skills mentioned earlier. You should also put down all your relevant work history. This includes any experience with animals, both domesticate and wild, and any other jobs that show off the key skills needed for becoming a zookeeper. Ask someone (a parent, friend, teacher, etc.) to review your resume so that you can make adjustments before sending it to a potential employer. If you need any help do not be afraid to ask! There are plenty of people that have experience writing resumes that will be more than happy to help. It is also important to note that many places want a cover letter too; I usually look up 'how to write a cober latter's on Google for help. There are many websites to help you better understand how to write resumes and cover letters.

49. FINDING A JOB

When trying to find a job a good starting point is to talk with your college; they may get an advanced notice of impending vacancies, especially if your school is known for there wildlife programs. On my schools website there was a job board where students could look up places that were hiring for full time, part time, seasonal, and internships. There are also various websites that you can use to search for a job, such as AZA or AAZK (these websites also allow you to look for internships). It is important to know that when you first start it may be difficult to find a full-time job. Apply for a seasonal position or a part time position and work your way up to full time.

50. BE FLEXIBLE

There are zoos all over the United States and throughout the world. You should widen your job search to a variety of locations that you are comfortable living in to get the best results. You need to be prepared for a potential move. Florida and Texas are the best U.S. states to look for starting zoo jobs, though that does not mean that you cannot find a position in another location. Remember that the zoo you start out at probably will not be the zoo you end up at.

BONUS TIPS

ANIMAL HEALTH

It is always helpful if you know and understand the basics of animal health. If you know common diseases that an animal can get you will be able to catch symptoms early on. Being able to catch symptoms early will give the animal a better chance at recovery and possibly prevent the disease from spreading to the other animals. Knowing diseases can also keep you safe since there are many zoonotic diseases that you could possibly catch, can pass to the animals, or even bring home and pass to your pets. One example of this is if you work with monkeys or apes you can pass on tuberculosis or they can give it to you. At the zoo I did my internship at, we needed to wear a face mask if we had a cold so we did not pass it on to the monkeys. It is important to note that at smaller zoos keepers usually rotate through working with the quaratine animals. Knowing and understanding animal health will be beneficial if you need to work with quaratine animals as a keeper.

UPDATED VACCINATIONS

When applying for keeper positions (or internships and externships) it is important to be up to date on all of your vaccinations. As mentioned in the previous tip, there are many zoonotic diseases that you can possibly come in contact with. It is important to be updated with your vaccines, so you limit the chance of catching a disease from an animal or passing one on. If you are not up to date, there is a chance that you will not get hired (most places ask for proof that you are updated on your vaccinations and for a negative TB test).

ENRICHMENT

Enrichment is defined as the act of improving or enhancing the quality or value of something. Knowing what enrichment does is important because it is a common question asked by zoo visitors. You should also know what types of enrichment works best for each animal in your care and you should understand what makes an enrichment item safe. Sensory enrichment is any enrichment that stimulates the animal's senses – visual, olfactory (smell), auditory (hearing), taste, and tactile (touch). Most enrichment is food based; this allows animals to display natural hunting/foraging behaviors rather than just giving them their food in a bowl. There are also manipulative toys. These are enrichment items that can be manipulated in some way via hands, mouth, legs, horns, or head for investigation and play. Environmental enrichment allows keepers to change or add complexity to the animal's environment. This is accomplished through swings, new substrates, climbing structures, hiding places, etc. Lastly, there is behavioral/social enrichment. This enrichment is interaction in the form of training and structured play.

A single piece of enrichment can fit into multiple of these categories. Enrichment helps stimulate an animal's mind and is extremely important in animals with high cognitive abilities such as monkey's and elephants. It is highly important to keep track of the enrichment you give so that the animal's do not become bored by getting the same enrichment every day. Make sure to change the enrichment every day and add different enrichment throughout the day (the monkeys at my zoo got enrichment three times a day).

You should also observe how the animals interact with the enrichment; what one species (or individual) loves another could hate! I leanred during my internship that the cotton top tamarins were very picky when it comes to enrichment. Most things they did not like at all and when they did use the enrichment we needed to hang it up really high in the exhibit since they did not like to go low to the ground. The Goeldi's monkeys were the only monkeys in our care that would go on the ground and use enrichment no matter where it was in the exhibit. Do not forget to take down enrichment at the end of the day that could potentially become dangerous without a keeper there to supervise! All enrichment with a rope was took down at the end of the day at my zoo.

FOCUS COURSES

It is important to take as many of the "-ology" (mammalogy, ornithology, herpetology, etc.) courses as possible. This will allow you to study many different animal species and not limit you to one type of animal. I personally took four of these courses and if given the chance would had loved to take more. See if your school offers these courses or if you can take them at another school. Do not be afraid to branch out and take a course you think you may not like; you might be surprised with how much you enjoy learning about a certain species. It is important to note that mammalogy tends to be the most poplar of these courses so do not be discouraged if you cannot take this course right away! I ended up taking ornithology before mammalogy because I could not fit it into my schedule like I originally planned.

DEALING WITH DIFFICULT GUESTS

In this career field it is common to deal with difficult people. There are many people who think all zoos/aquariums are bad and it is your job to professionally debate and tell them why that is not true. Not only will these people come to the zoo, but you will see comments on the internet and hear people talking about your career choice in a negative light whenever it is brought up. From my experience there is someone in my family who does not like zoos that I constantly debate and someone at the zoo that I did my internship at who was always there trying to persuade the visitors that we were not a good zoo. One of the keepers I worked with even told me about how when she went to the hospital still in her work clothes a nurse told her that she did not like zoos and that the animals should stay in the wild. This is very prevalent when you are a keeper and you need to be sure of yourself and this job so that you can defend your career. Always make sure to stay professional and do not be discouraged if you cannot change their mind! Most of the time you will not be able to get them to agree with you no matter what you say or how many times you say it.

COMPETITIVE

Something that you should always keep in mind is that zookeeping is a very competitive job. Some of my friends have said that they applied to over 25 places to find a job zookeeping and some are still looking! There are only so many positions available so working your hardest, starting early, and gaining as much experience as possible can only be beneficial to you. Do not let this discourage you though! If you are passionate and dedicated, you will get the job of your dreams somewhere down the road. If you love something enough you will find a way to reach your goals in the end.

DEALING WITH DEATH

Working with live animals means that you will unfortunately deal with animal deaths. Working closely with the animals in your care means that you form bonds with the animals. When they get old and can no longer have a good quality of life, they get euthanized. This is just like losing a beloved pet; it is never easy to euthanize an animal that you care for, but it is something that needs to be dealt with often in this career field.

COMPASSION FATIGUE

The simple way to describe compassion fatigue is that it is the cost of caring. Being a zookeeper (especially working in rehabilitation where you deal with death every day) can way heavily on you. It is a very demanding job and it can cause you to burnout. Dealing with animal death or working long hours, weekends, and/or holidays can drive people to the breaking point. It is important for keepers to understand the symptoms of compassion fatigue so that if they or a coworker starts showing signs, they can get the help they need. Symptoms of compassion fatigue include difficulty concentrating, intrusive imagery, feeling discouraged about the world, hopelessness, exhaustion and irritability, high attrition, and negative outcomes. If you or someone you know show any of these signs make sure to reach out to a professional doctor and/or therapist to get properly treated.

WHY ZOOS ARE IMPORTANT

If you have decided that becoming a zookeeper is the career for you it is important to understand why zoos are important because there will be many people who will debate that zoos should not exist (as mentioned previously). Keeping animals in captivity allows us the chance to learn about them in a way that we cannot in the wild. Learning about the animal's behaviors in captivity will help us conserve and manage wild populations. Zoos also raise money for conservation efforts for numerous species and ecosystems. Zoos are a great source of education for the public; in 2014 700 million people visited zoos worldwide and this number stays pretty consistent throughout the years. There is a breeding program called the species survival plan that breeds endangered species in the hopes to reintroduce them into the wild in the future. Some captive breeding programs have already been extremely successful (Black footed ferrets and the California condor to name a few).

NEVER GIVE UP!

This last tip may sound cheesy, but it is very true! If zookeeping is something you are truly passionate about then as long as you continuously work towards your goal you will get there! It may be difficult at times, and zookeeping may not be the most glamorous job but as long as you love animals and want to care for them this job can be extremely rewarding. I can honestly say, from just my short time in the field, this career is everything I could have hoped for and more. There are tough days, just like there would be in any job, but being able to see the animals that I care for will never fail to bring a smile to my face.

OTHER HELPFUL RESOURCES (SUCH AS WEBSITES).

Association of Zoos and Aquariums (AZA) https://www.aza.org/

American Association of Zookeepers (AAZK) https://aazk.org/

World Association of Zoos and Aquariums (WAZA) https://www.waza.org/

Zoological Association of America (ZAA) https://zaa.org/

Global Federation of Animal Sanctuaries https://www.sanctuaryfederation.org/

READ OTHER

50 THINGS TO KNOW

BOOKS

50 Things to Know

Stay up to date with new releases on Amazon:
https://amzn.to/2VPNGr7

Mailing List: Join the 50 Things to Know
Mailing List to Learn About New Releases

50 Things to Know

Please leave your honest review of this book on Amazon and Goodreads. We appreciate your positive and constructive feedback. Thank you.

Made in the USA
Middletown, DE
26 March 2024